AMISTAD

AMISTAD

A FILM BY
Steven Spielberg

A JUNIOR NOVEL BY
Joyce Annette Barnes

BASED ON THE SCREENPLAY BY
David Franzoni

For David

PUFFIN BOOKS
Published by the Penguin Group
Penguin Putnam Inc., 375 Hudson Street, New York,
New York 10014, U.S.A.
Penguin Books Ltd, 27 Wrights Lane, London W8 5TZ, England
Penguin Books Australia Ltd, Ringwood, Victoria, Australia
Penguin Books Canada Ltd, 10 Alcorn Avenue, Toronto, Ontario,
Canada M4V 3B2
Penguin Books (N.Z.) Ltd, 182-190 Wairau Road, Auckland 10,
New Zealand

Penguin Books Ltd, Registered Offices: Harmondsworth, Middlesex,
England

First published in the United States of America by Puffin Books,
a member of Penguin Putnam Inc., 1997

3 5 7 9 10 8 6 4 2

ISBN 0-14-039063-4

Printed in the United States of America
Set in Garamond

Acknowledgments

I would like to thank Cindy Kane for recommending me for this project and Ellen Stamper at Puffin Books for all her hard work and diligence in editing the manuscript and helping me complete this book. Thanks also to Mary Jack Wald for being such a great advocate. Finally, I want to thank Ms. Debbie Allen for her valuable input and words of encouragement.

I

In the dank hold of the *Amistad,* as the ship pitched in stormy winds, Cinque lay on the splintering deck shackled in chains. Above him came the sounds of running feet and frantic voices, muffled by the rain—the crew trying to navigate the low black schooner through choppy seas.

Cinque didn't understand their words. He didn't care about the wind and the rain. All of his attention, and all the strength remaining after months at sea as a captive of the white slave traders, focused on one rusty spike lodged in a rotting plank. It was unbearably hot in the four-foot-high slave hold. His sweat—and his blood—from his glistening black skin slid onto the metal shaft and soaked into the wood, loosening the stubborn spike millimeter by millimeter.

A quick flash of lightning in the night sky, a

final desperate pull, and the nail came loose. Cinque jabbed the metal into the iron lock of his neck manacle, twisting it left and right until, finally, the lock gave way.

And then he was free.

He released the others, released the fury the forty-nine young Africans had stored since being kidnapped from their homes in Sierra Leone and sold into slavery. Like fierce lions loosed from captivity, they surged behind their leader onto the ship's top deck into the storm.

The first man they met had no chance to defend himself, much less warn the others. With one blow, Cinque struck him down and impaled the man with his own cutlass. Next, the Africans breached a storeroom door and seized rows of long, heavy knives, with wide blades sharpened to perfection. Uttering cries of anger and revenge, they set out to find the rest of the ship's crew.

The big Temne warrior Yamba strangled the startled scream of another sailor. Fala, a small, brown man with teeth as sharp as a piranha's, attacked the Creole cook. Only days before, the cook had taunted Cinque and the other captives, making them believe they were to be chopped up and eaten once they reached their destination.

Now, the Creole cook looked into the face of

death as Fala bared his teeth and raised his thirty-two-inch blade before him. Big and defiant, the cook aimed his meat cleaver in defense, but seconds later, he screamed in agony as small, quick Fala chopped off his hand with the knife.

The ones called Ruiz and Montes, the ones who had bought them as slaves at an auction in Havana, fled below deck. Cinque let them go—for the moment. Instead, he ordered his Mende brothers to go after two other sailors and the ship's captain who were trying to escape by lifeboat. The two sailors got away, dropping into the raging waters. But the sea, as if an ally of the angry men, swallowed the small boat.

Captain Ferrer's path, however, was blocked. He slashed frantically, fatally wounding the first two men to advance. That left him face-to-face with the powerful Cinque.

Cinque did not understand the other man's words, but the message in his eyes spoke clearly enough. Captain Ferrer meant to fight for his life. Cinque meant to kill.

They locked swords, the blades lit by a lightning flash. The captain was strong, but Cinque was younger and stronger. His blade cut easily through the captain's defense. Ferrer fell to his knees, pleading for his life.

These words, from the man who had piloted him away from freedom, meant nothing to Cinque. He drove his sabre through the captain's heart.

Cinque now turned to the others. "The two who claim to own us have hidden themselves," he said. "Find them."

2

"I say we kill them both," Cinque told Yamba the next morning as they stood on the bloodied deck contemplating the fate of the only two remaining white men on board. Cinque had chained Ruiz and Montes to a rail along the boat's stern. Now he kept a sharp eye on the two—the young Ruiz, bold, brazen, even in irons, and the pale, trembling Montes, who nursed his bleeding head wound and lame arm, battle scars from the night before. He and Yamba talked only a few yards away.

"We can sail this ship home by ourselves."

Yamba dismissed Cinque's plan with a quick shake of his large, shaved head. "You know nothing about sailing. And neither does anyone else here— but those two. We need their help."

Cinque's eyes narrowed as he watched Ruiz and Montes draw back from the Kissi warrior Fala. His thoughts were at war. Perhaps Yamba was right. None of the Africans had any experience with sailing vessels, and they had no idea where they were or how far away from home they had traveled. But Cinque knew this much—for months, they had sailed away from the rising sun. So home must be in that direction. Besides, he didn't trust the two men.

Yamba remained convinced, and Cinque certainly wanted no trouble with *him.* He reluctantly agreed.

As he approached the two men, he lifted his sabre toward the sunrise and spoke to them in Mende. He pointed toward the rising sun and motioned for Ruiz to turn the boat around.

The other man nodded, as if he understood Cinque's gestures.

Ruiz then reluctantly took hold of the helm and slowly inched the ship around to begin the long journey east.

◆ ◆ ◆

Though he had been a fearless leader during their revolt against the Spanish crew, Cinque was a reluctant captain now. After all, before being kidnapped, he had been a rice farmer in his Mende village. The son of the richest farmer, yes, but he had never been near a ship, let alone sailed one. He knew nothing of navigation, of raising sails, of keeping fed and content fifty-three other souls.

Dressed in white pantaloons, a red kerchief around his neck, and sabre hanging from his waist, Cinque swung himself back and forth from a halyard. But his eyes were troubled by what he had seen the night before.

By day, he could keep careful watch over Ruiz and Montes, whom he did not trust. They talked too much to each other—in a language foreign to the Africans. Cinque knew the power of a common language. Hadn't he convinced his fellow brothers to mutiny by holding secret *poro* council meetings in their native Mende tongue, beyond the comprehension of the whites.

What deception or treachery might Ruiz and Montes have planned?

By day, Ruiz kept the *Amistad* sailing eastward, toward Africa. Of that, Cinque was sure. Last night, however, as Cinque dozed on deck, he'd been awakened by a sudden strange shift in the flapping of the sails and a whirling around of the stars above his head. What did this mean?

He accosted Ruiz at the helm, pointed to the stars and spoke in Mende.

Ruiz acted as if he did not understand.

Cinque stared at the navigational equipment and

7

maps and then looked suspiciously back to Ruiz. He lifted his sabre to Ruiz's neck, the gesture saying, "You'd better not be trying to deceive me."

Angrily, Ruiz released the wheel, challenging Cinque to sail the ship himself.

The wheel spun wildly. The sky reeled again, and the ship lurched to one side. In their separate tribal encampments, marked off by colored sticks, the Africans tumbled into one another. Montes, asleep on deck, banged his head against a wall.

Cinque grabbed the wheel and steadied the stars. He felt the power in his hand as the sailing boat responded to the movements of the helm. The sails billowed full with wind. The ship moved forward confidently.

But to where?

Clearly panicked, Ruiz seized the wheel again. Cinque let him have it, though now, he was even more suspicious that the ship was no longer headed toward Africa.

Cinque suspected, but he could prove nothing.

The next night, Cinque tried to convince Yamba that something was wrong. But Yamba, even when he observed the stars turning above him, was unconcerned. "You worry too much about unimportant things," Yamba said to him and walked away. Yamba had taken to donning the captain's hat, and with it the self-importance of a self-appointed leader. Cinque watched the big Temne warily and with a little disdain.

There were four children on board—the boy, Kale, two little girls, Teme and Kene, and Maseray, an older girl, almost a woman. Cinque felt for them most. He had comforted them when they cried, hungry and sick, during the long voyage from Africa on the larger slave ship. He had steadied them when it was time to fight for freedom onboard the smaller vessel, the *Amistad*. He had even joked with them once the danger was over. Now, the food supply was diminishing and the water was almost gone. Africa was nowhere in sight—no land at all.

For long, sweltering days, then weeks, they drifted on the open sea.

3

Some nights the sea was calm. The other Africans, believing they were sailing back—to their loved ones, their farms, their businesses, their freedom—gathered in camps on deck to tell stories in their native dialects. Boastful Yamba held court among his Temne tribesmen. Buakei, a young Mende man, and Maseray passed romantic looks back and forth. Cinque alone noticed the moon sail port to starboard as the ship changed direction *again*.

Then, in the distance, he saw a light.

"Quiet," he commanded the others.

It was a ship, drifting into and out of sight through the fog.

With sabre and musket in hand, Cinque pushed his former captors away from the helm and chained them to a rail. He blew out the oil-fired lights and stood guard as the ship approached.

The one called Montes had spotted the ship also. Cinque heard him whispering to Ruiz and caught just a glimpse of Ruiz shoving something between the wooden slats to the deck below.

Cinque glared at the two white men. "Ssss," Ruiz hissed to Montes.

They were up to something, but Cinque's first concern was the oncoming vessel.

It was a large white boat, ferrying finely dressed passengers along the calm waters to the sound of music. As it drew closer, Cinque tied off the wheel and placed the muzzle of his gun to Ruiz's head. "Ssss," Cinque warned, imitating the white men.

The ships passed within yards of each other through the fog. Music drifted across on the wind, but otherwise, there was no sound. The two ships sailed on like ghost ships in a midnight dream.

◆ ◆ ◆

More weeks passed, yet there was still no sight of home. The ragged sails hung almost useless on their wooden poles. Cinque could see that barnacles and sea grass clung to the sides of the ship. The last of the drinking water had been poured into two clay jugs, and Cinque had reduced rations to half a cup a day. The other Africans had become anxious, irritable, mad with thirst.

11

They challenged Cinque's authority. When, they wanted to know, would they reach their homes?

Then, one day, Fala spotted land through a thick mist of fog. *"Ndogboe!"* he shouted. Home! The others peered across the water, saw the silhouette of a shoreline, and broke into shouts of jubilation. Cinque, looking toward the distant horizon, was not so sure as the others.

He signaled to his Mende brother Buakei and to Yamba that they must go ashore and check about.

With Buakei, Fala (who insisted on going), Yamba, and a few of his Temne brothers, Cinque stepped from the lifeboat onto a narrow, rocky beach of the long shoreline. They entered the woods to look for a spring and fill their jugs. After that, Cinque had decided, they must reboard the ship and continue on.

He had no idea where they were, but of one thing he was sure: this was not home.

4

Once on shore, Cinque and the others found more than they expected.

As they filled their water jugs at a stream hidden from the road by thick shrubbery, they heard a strange clattery-clacking sound. Peeking through the bushes, they were amazed at the sight of a man, black like them, sailing by on a strange, wheeled contraption. They followed him from a safe distance, keeping out of sight, and came upon a grand estate peopled with other blacks—from some strange land where they wore too many clothes and where even the grown men's faces were bereft of the symbolic gris-gris markings.

Buakei pointed to a dignified figure perched in the driver's seat of a coach. "He must be *a ngie* here," he said to Cinque.

Cinque nodded, but he had some doubt about

whether the man sitting there was the "big man," the one in charge. He observed two stately women who were gathering flowers in a garden change into bowing servants when a white woman emerged from the house. The "big man" on the coach snapped to attention as an older white man climbed into the carriage. Cinque understood immediately who the "big man" was.

"Let's get out of here," he said.

Carrying their jugs full of water, they headed back toward the shore. But they stopped in their tracks when they saw a large ship in full sail bearing down on the *Amistad.*

The Africans rushed to their lifeboats and rowed furiously back to the ship, ready to fight once again, if they must, for their freedom.

◆ ◆ ◆

Wild-looking Fala perched on the prow of the lifeboat. He shouted war cries at the men who sped toward them in longboats dropped from the larger ship. The sight of Cinque, Yamba, and especially Fala clearly astounded these new sailors, but they recovered quickly enough to begin firing their muskets.

Beyond, Cinque saw other longboats headed toward the *Amistad.* Two Africans onboard the

14

Amistad hoisted the anchor out of the water. The ship immediately lurched forward as the wind hit its sails. "Row harder," Cinque commanded his brothers on the lifeboat. If they could reach the *Amistad* before the pursuing sailors, they might be able to escape.

But the gunshots continued. Bullets flew past the African men like sharp sparks of fire. Fala hurled an oar at one of the longboats, hitting a sailor in the chest. But a volley of shots answered his attack. Panicking, Buakei, Fala, Yamba, and the others leaped into the water, hoping to swim back to shore. Cinque dove in after them. He headed not for the shoreline, but instead to the open sea. He meant to swim back to Africa, if he could. Or to his death. Death was better than once again becoming a prisoner.

His muscled arms and strong strokes carried him forcefully through the water. Still, he sensed the pursuers upon him. Was there no escape? Just as they came close enough to pluck him out of the water, Cinque dove under the surface and disappeared.

He pulled through the water, swimming further and further into its depths. His lungs began to burn, but he had given up hope of returning home above the ocean waters. He would return the way so many others had before him, in spirit only.

Suddenly, a voice—faint, mournful—called to him through the murky water. A Mende chant.

The voice was a woman's, his wife's, calling him back. But how could that be?

She pleaded with him to return, return to the surface of the water and live! Cinque tried to ignore the voice, but her wailing followed him down.

Think of me. Think of your three children. Think of your village, your farm, your family. There is still a chance you can return to us—alive.

A little further down, a few more strokes, and there would be no such return. Cinque's lungs screamed in protest, and his heart twisted from the sound of Tafe's chant. Her cries finally overcame his resolve to die. He turned in the water and clawed frantically for the surface, emerging in a thunderous splash just as his lungs were about to burst. Blinded at first by the sun, Cinque soon distinguished the muzzles of muskets aimed at his head.

5

"I'm Lieutenant Commander Gedney of the U.S. Naval ship *Washington*. Where is your captain?"

The Africans did not appear to understand his words; they did not answer.

From below, two white men appeared, bedraggled, still manacled. They fell to their knees at Gedney's feet, crying out in Spanish.

Gedney and his second in command, Meade, neither of whom spoke Spanish, were unsure what to make of these two. Then a sailor emerged from the slave deck, a handkerchief pressed to his mouth. Reeling, he called out weakly, "Sir?" Gedney followed his gaze, knelt down, and glared into the rancid hold.

Retreating quickly, he turned to Meade, now understanding everything. His look was one of comprehension and not a little bit of delight. This was a slave ship—the hold had carried these Africans as its cargo. Slaves could be sold for a lot of money in America, especially strong ones like some of those captured here. And as "rescuers" of the two slave owners, Meade and Gedney stood a chance of claiming at least some of the cash. The laws of salvage guaranteed that.

"Make sure those chains are secure," he instructed a sailor. "Then set sail for Connecticut. We'll let an American court settle this matter."

◆ ◆ ◆

Shackled together, the Africans were marched by torchlight along the water and into the town. There, they stood before an old stone building, shivering from cold and fear. Some of them wore festive garments from the ship's cargo hold. Some of them wore very little clothing at all.

Townspeople stared at them as if they were creatures from another world. They looked with pity on the children. But Cinque saw fear and disgust in their eyes as they gawked at Fala and his sharpened teeth, gleaming in the moonlight, and the big Temne Yamba who towered over the rest of them.

They consider us murderers, Cinque thought, or worse—beasts who must be destroyed. Yet, he would not let them see the fear that shook his every nerve, or the sadness that overwhelmed his every thought. Cinque suffered their scornful looks as an honorable Mende man would. He faced the townspeople with his eyes steady and his head held high.

◆ ◆ ◆

Once inside the prison, Cinque fought his new captors, but they beat him into submission and threw him into the jail cell with the others. The young African girls were led to a separate cell across a muddy courtyard. They cried out to Cinque, their "father," as they were led away. His heart seemed to shrivel up inside him.

The guards left them there. As their torchlights faded away, Cinque got a last look at the crushed souls imprisoned along with him. He thought of the two brothers who had been killed in the initial revolt. Eight more had died from hunger and disease during the weeks when they thought they were heading toward home. Now, they were captives again. His revolt had been a failure.

In the gloom of the American prison, out of view of the people in the town, Cinque finally hung his head in despair.

6

Across the Atlantic Ocean, in the royal house of Spain, Queen Isabella II, wearing her diamond tiara, sat at the elegantly prepared table in the dining room of the palace. Servants stood close by, ready to do her bidding. Did she need more jam spread on her bread? More juice in her goblet?

Isabella was only nine. She had been only three years old when she had been declared queen of Spain. Now, six years later, she was already bored with it all.

So when General Espartero interrupted her solitary breakfast with the ominous words, "Something has happened," Isabella refused to look up to acknowledge she'd even heard him.

Maybe, she thought, as she scraped her silverware against the expensive china plate, *if I ignore him, whatever it is will just go away.*

◆ ◆ ◆

On the other side of the Atlantic, United States president Martin Van Buren smiled and waved to the cheering crowd in a small Pennsylvania town. Above him fluttered a banner proclaiming, RE-ELECT VAN BUREN. GOD BLESS AMERICA! But Van Buren's smile dropped when his secretary, Leder Hammond, shouted some disturbing news in his ear.

"What?" the president asked, wondering why he must be interrupted *now.*

◆ ◆ ◆

Later, in his train car headed back to Washington, D.C., Van Buren listened impassively to a Spanish emissary's complaint.

"The schooner was conveying the slaves from Havana to Puerto Principe when the attack occurred," Señor Calderon explained. Calderon had been ordered to America by the nine-year-old queen.

"Uh-huh," the president replied, throwing a look at Hammond.

"They killed everyone on board but two courageous men who eventually managed to draw the attention of the American survey brig *Washington* to their plight," Calderon said.

"Uh-huh," Van Buren said again.

21

The Spanish emissary continued. "These slaves belong to Señors Montes and Ruiz, and, in the larger sense, to Spain. On behalf of Her Majesty, Queen Isabella II, I must insist on their prompt return."

The president glanced at his secretary. He was much too busy for this kind of thing. To Calderon, he asked, "Would you excuse us a moment?"

Nodding discreetly, the Spanish gentleman took his leave.

"Hammond, this is a Cuban vessel he's talking about?" Van Buren asked.

"Yes, sir," the secretary replied, "the *Amistad*. It's Spanish for 'friendship.'"

Van Buren rubbed his brow and frowned. *Maybe if I ignore him, he will just go away.*

"Leder," he said, "I'm trying to drink my brandy after a very long day. There are what—four million Negroes in this country? Why on earth should I concern myself with these forty-three?"

Hammond lowered his eyes. He understood.

"I don't care how you do it," Van Buren told him, lighting his fine cigar. "Just take care of it."

7

News of the *Amistad* rebellion and the prisoners now held in a New Haven jail spread from town to town by sensational newspapers like the one Theodore Joadson held in his hand. The large banner headline read, MASSACRE AT SEA!

Joadson had been a slave. Now, he was a distinguished New Haven scholar and an active participant in the anti-slavery movement. He read the newspaper story and knew immediately that there was another side to be told. The accused prisoners would have few friends on their side. He left his small rooms immediately and headed toward the docks to find his friend and fellow abolitionist, Lewis Tappan.

Joadson spotted Tappan talking to other prosperous businessmen in front of Tappan's thriving silk warehouse. Joadson could not hear what they said, and he did not interrupt or even acknowledge Tappan. Though both men were dedicated to the anti-slavery cause, they also knew it was sometimes wise to keep their abolitionist sentiments between themselves. Joadson instead handed the newspaper to a nearby dockworker and asked him to deliver it to Tappan.

Immediately upon reading it, Tappan ended his business conversation and joined Joadson on the dock. They walked to a nearby church, their heads bent in serious discussion. As they climbed to the attic of the church, the steeple clock chimed the hour. The sound was deafening, but the two men barely noticed, so engrossed were they in their conversation. They crossed the busy newsroom of the abolitionist paper Tappan published, the clanging of the church bell now joined by the noise of a hand-run press.

"The *Amistad* is too small to be a transatlantic slaver," said Joadson.

Tappan sat down at a desk. "Then the men must be plantation slaves? From the West Indies, perhaps?"

"They don't look it. I caught a glimpse of them on their way to jail. Several have these"—Joadson drew lines across his cheek—"scars."

Tappan glanced at the headline again. He was a wealthy silk merchant, yes, but he was also an

24

impassioned abolitionist who could not help but be moved by the Africans' plight.

"They will be charged with murder, no doubt," Joadson said gravely.

"Then we must provide for their defense," Tappan replied.

A pressworker handed Joadson a fresh copy of their latest edition. The headline for this newspaper read: FREEDOM FIGHT AT SEA!

◆ ◆ ◆

Still shackled, Cinque and the others trudged once again through the cold, gray streets. Some of them were now wrapped in coarse blankets that only partially hid their chains. They did not know where they were headed, but Cinque felt something important was to happen that day. Maybe on this day they would be set free to return to their homes. Or maybe they were on their way to be killed.

Along the way, they passed an elegantly dressed black man driving a carriage. Amazed at the sight, one Mende man called, *"Marda!"* The coachman did not even blink.

Buakei must have remembered his mistaking a servant for the "big man" on the shoreline plantation. He corrected his friend. "No, Kimbo. He is not a chief."

25

"Then he must be a chief's advisor," Kimbo said. *"Mori! Maha!"*

The coachman remained deaf to his summons.

"No brother," Buakei sighed. "He isn't that, either."

"Ndeha! Nadiama!" the man tried again. "Surely, this man is our brother."

Buakei again shook his head.

"What is he then?" Kimbo wanted to know.

Buakei was not sure. Cinque, however, supplied the answer. "He is a *'pu-mui.'*" A white man, he said with disdain as they filed past the coachman who refused to even look their way.

◆ ◆ ◆

To the young man in gold spectacles who stood against the back wall, the prisoners appeared odd and uncomfortable splayed along a wooden bench in the New Haven courtroom. The defendants were charged with murder and other crimes. Behind them, row after row of seats held curious men and women. Most of the spectators were white, but a few black faces gleamed among them.

The court crier sounded his pike and announced: "Hear-ye, hear-ye! For the Commonwealth of Connecticut, in the capital of Hartford–New Haven, and for the District Court of the United States of

26

America, in the year of our Lord eighteen hundred and thirty-nine—the Honorable Andrew T. Judson presiding. All rise!"

The prisoners, the young man noted, did not stand.

Judge Judson, his black robe billowing around him, took his place at the bench without comment.

Immediately, the United States prosecutor William Holabird rose to speak. "Your Honor, if it please the court—"

He pointed dramatically to the bemused defendants, these men who appeared before the judge with no one to represent them and no way to speak for themselves.

"I charge these slaves with piracy and murder—"

"Your Honor!" a voice interrupted from the crowded gallery. Lewis Tappan emerged, waving papers before the judge. "On behalf of these *men,* I present this petition."

Holabird sneered at the rude interruption. "I was speaking, Your Honor. If Mr. Tappan would kindly refrain from *impersonating* a lawyer, I will continue—"

But his charges were cut short once again, as a policeman pushed the crowd aside and two distinguished-looking gentlemen strode into the room. The first one was the imperious Señor Calderon, the

27

Spanish ambassador. The other, a tall American, caused a stir among the gathering. Even Judge Judson looked unprepared for the appearance of Mr. John Forsyth, the U.S. secretary of state.

The man at the back of the room grinned as he serenely watched the growing confusion.

"The slaves, Your Honor," Secretary Forsyth intoned, "are by rights the property of Spain, and are to be returned to her *posthaste*—"

"Them slaves belong to me and my mate!" a third interrupter declared. All heads swung back in the direction of two American navy lieutenants. One of the lieutenants produced an unofficial-looking document and read:

"We, Thomas R. Gedney and Richard W. Meade, do hereby claim salvage on the high seas of the Spanish ship *Amistad* and all her cargo. Including slaves!"

Judge Judson regarded Lt. Gedney's papers with eyebrows raised. Secretary of State Forsyth laughed outright.

"You are making this claim over that of the queen of Spain?" Judson asked.

"Well, where was *she* when we was fightin' the wind to bring that ship in?" Gedney wanted to know.

The spectators laughed. Objections spewed forth

28

from all the attorneys. The judge banged his mallet for order. Through gritted teeth, he asked, "Is there anyone *else* present I need to hear from?"

A lone voice answered. "Your Honor, here are the true owners of these slaves."

Another attorney. This one representing Señors Ruiz and Montes, the Cuban planters. They, too, demanded possession of the prisoners. Judge Judson, looking down into the crowded room, sighed heavily. He must have wondered how this matter had become so complicated—how his proceedings had turned into a farce.

The most amused by it all was the man at the back of the room, the young lawyer Roger S. Baldwin.

To him, it was all so simple.

8

Cinque left the courtroom with a low opinion of American *poros*. Unlike the dignified meetings of his Mende brothers at home, this one was unruly and unproductive. He would not look up for the curious people who lined the halls just to get a glimpse of the "murderers." But Cinque's eyes lingered on one man, one with wildly curled yellow hair and small gold eyeglasses. There was something different about him, Cinque thought, but what?

◆ ◆ ◆

In the hall of the courthouse, Baldwin boldly stepped up to Lewis Tappan, introduced himself, and presented his card.

"A real-estate attorney?" Tappan asked skeptically. His eyes moved from the young man's cheap suit to his scuffed shoes, unruly curls, and snide smile. Tappan looked briefly at Joadson, a question in his glance.

Baldwin continued to smile. "I get people's property back for them, Mr. Tappan. Or sometimes I get it taken *away*. I'd like to help you."

He waited for the two men to get his point. They didn't.

"Clearly this is a property issue. All of the claims"—Baldwin gestured back toward the courtroom—"speak to the issue of ownership."

Tappan cut Baldwin off with a wave of his hand. He thanked Baldwin perfunctorily. "I'm afraid what's needed here is a criminal attorney."

Baldwin shook his head. "If that were the way to go, I wouldn't have bothered coming over here. Would I have." He turned around and walked away.

It was not a question, but a challenge.

9

Exhausted by captivity and the confusing day in court, Cinque tried to sleep.

He lay on the hard, narrow cot, a thin blanket his only protection against the cold night air. Cinque closed his eyes, wanting to shut out the sight of their wretched conditions—the thick, closely set bars, the dark cement walls, the downcast looks on the faces of the others. He hoped for a few hours of sleep, of escape. But Buakei wanted to talk.

"I don't think anything was decided in there today, do you?"

Cinque sighed, his eyes half closed. "It took a lot of people to not decide anything."

Some of the Africans had settled into their now familiar routines. A few men played Mende poker with small articles of clothing. A group of Kono listened to a *griot*, the historian of the group, telling stories. Fala, the lone Kissi among the Africans, crouched in a corner and searched around the dirt floor. He kept himself apart from the scornful looks of the others.

Buakei, as he talked to Cinque, stared longingly past his bars toward Maseray, who huddled under a thin blanket a courtyard away. So it was he who first noticed the visitors. "What's this? Another council so late at night?"

Cinque sat up.

A nearby Temne scoffed at the idea. "Don't be stupid, Mende. Look how they are dressed." All eyes fell on the hushed, wary guests who had come out at night in their tall hats and fancy clothing. "They're obviously *entertainers.*"

More Africans looked beyond their bars. They sat quietly, expectantly. Cinque wondered what kind of show this group would present.

Moments passed, but no words. The two groups watched each other. Cinque recognized one man— the overweight jailer who looked to Cinque like one who ate heartily but who gave little more than rice and water to his African prisoners.

The fat man gestured a warning to the ladies in the group. When he moved, coins jingled in his pockets.

Cinque's face grew hot. He realized that the

people were not entertainers, but *spectators* brought there by the jailer to get a glimpse of the "African cannibals."

"Why are they just *standing* there?" a Mende asked.

"Be still and maybe they'll begin," Kimbo replied.

Only Fala moved.

"Kissi!" Buakei hissed at him, urging him to be still.

A minute of more watching passed.

"They're boring," a Mende told his brothers.

Buakei urged, "Ssss—"

But Fala had already lost interest and, anyway, he had found what he had been searching for . . . the perfect stone. Into the quiet came a scraping sound. All eyes turned toward Fala—who sat calmly in his corner, sharpening his teeth with the rock.

Both groups gasped and stared at him in horror and disgust.

Beast! the Americans must have thought.

"Stupid Kissi," a Temne groaned. "Why must we be locked up with the likes of *him?*"

10

The 72-year-old ex-president pretended to be asleep. He sat in his seat in the U.S. House of Representatives with his eyes closed, his bald head bowed, plump hands resting across his pot belly.

He had listened for hours as the representative from South Carolina criticized his proposal to establish a Smithsonian Institute. Like many others present that day, he had grown bored with the long-winded remarks.

John Quincy Adams had been the sixth President of the United States. Now, he was a congressman from Massachusetts. He was known to his colleagues as "Old Man Eloquent," but he had grown cantankerous and impatient of late.

Most days, he just felt old. His hand shook when he wrote, his eyes watered incessantly, he suffered from rheumatism and lumbago, and daily, his memory failed.

"Who?" he asked absently when his congressional aide informed him of visitors requesting to see him after the session ended.

"Lewis Tappan, sir, along with a colored man."

"Do I know this Mr. . . . ?" Adams had already forgotten his name.

The aide, weighed down with papers, sighed sympathetically.

"Yes, sir, you do. You have met him on . . . countless occasions."

◆ ◆ ◆

Adams shook Tappan's hand warmly when they met in the gardens planted right outside of the domed Capitol. Yet he could not recall ever having met the man. Adams wondered what business had brought these two men all the way from New Haven, Connecticut, to see him. Something about a slave rebellion on the high seas. Arrests. A trial.

"This case has great significance, sir," the man called Tappan was saying. "Our secretary of state, on behalf of the president, supports the queen of Spain in her claims that the Africans belong to her. And there are others—"

Adams abruptly interrupted. "Do you really think

36

Van Buren cares about the whims of a nine-year-old girl in a tiara?" Adams pointed toward the White House, which they could not see. "Having been there, I know—only one thing occupies his thoughts this time of year. Getting himself re-elected."

The old politician knelt among the foliage and rummaged among the flowers. He had already decided to turn down their request for his involvement in the case. "Gentlemen, I'm neither friend nor foe to the abolitionist cause. No, I won't help you."

He clipped a cutting from one of the plants, looking around to ensure no one had caught him in the act.

Joadson, who had been silent until now, spoke up.

"Sir, I know you," Joadson said, ignoring Tappan's frowning expression. "I know about your presidency. And your father's."

Adams lifted his eyebrows at the mention of his father.

"You were a child at his side when he helped invent America. But there remains one task still left undone—crushing slavery. Your record confirms you're an abolitionist, President Adams, even if you won't. You belong with us."

Tappan looked horrified at Joadson's impropriety. Adams, however, controlled his indignation.

"You are quite the scholar, aren't you, Mr. Joadson? But let me tell you something about that quality. Without at least one tenth its measure in grace, such education is worthless. Take it from someone who knows. Excuse me, gentlemen." He rose to leave.

"Sir, we aimed high coming to see you," Tappan implored.

"Aim lower," Adams said as he walked away with his little clipping in hand.

II

"I don't care about the fence. Tear it down," Baldwin said as he led a man and his two goats out of his crowded New Haven law office.

"He'll just put up another one," the farmer said.

"And you'll tear it down. And the one after that. You are completely within your rights."

Joadson and Tappan watched the farmer take his goats out the door. They stood against a wall, feeling out of place in the dingy waiting room.

Baldwin surveyed the room, no doubt trying to decide which client to see next.

A large woman nursed her baby in one seat. A whaler with a crudely shaped ivory fist where his hand should have been sat in another. An old mountain man paced back and forth. Finally, Baldwin's eyes fell on Tappan and Joadson. Baldwin nodded slightly and gave them his now-familiar

39

snide smile. It seemed to say, "I knew you'd come to see me sooner or later."

The two abolitionists had set their sights on a lawyer much more highly placed than Roger Baldwin. They needed someone of national stature to take up the cause of the ill-treated Africans. John Quincy Adams had been such a man, but he was only the first to decline the job. In the weeks since their return from Washington, D.C., Joadson and Tappan had asked no less than four other prominent attorneys to take the case. All four had politely refused.

Baldwin was their last—maybe their only—choice.

"Mr. Gutwillig," Baldwin called to the man with the ivory fist, making it clear that the two abolitionists would have to wait their turn.

♦ ♦ ♦

Over a fish dinner later in a seedy wharfside tavern, Joadson spoke on the matter before them. "If the courts award them to Spain, they'll be sent to Cuba to be executed. If those two lieutenants prevail, they'll most likely sell them back to Spain, where they'll be executed."

"What are they worth to you?" Baldwin interrupted. He addressed Tappan, who had been staring at his dinner, which appeared to stare back.

40

"You needn't worry about the fish here. It's fresh." Baldwin took a mouthful to make his point and spoke as he chewed. "Now, about the case. It's much simpler than you think, Mr. Joadson. It's like land, livestock, heirlooms, what-have-you. Determine who the rightful owner is, and victory draws within spitting distance."

The frown on Tappan's face deepened. "Livestock?" he huffed, indignant.

"The only way one may legally sell or purchase slaves is if they are born slaves. Right?"

With some hesitation, Joadson agreed.

Despite the 1808 U.S. law that banned the transportation of any more Africans as slaves into the country, the slave trade had continued to flourish.

"So are they?" Baldwin asked.

"We very much doubt it," Joadson replied. He was not as skeptical as Tappan about Roger S. Baldwin. He was willing to listen to the young man's ideas.

"Let's say," Baldwin continued, "that they are Cuban slaves. Then, they are mere possessions and no more deserving of a criminal trial than a bookcase or a plow. And we can all go home."

Tappan's appetite for the man had about reached his limit. Joadson glanced to his friend, pleading for patience.

41

"Let's say, on the other hand, that they aren't Cuban slaves. Or anybody's slaves. That they've been kidnapped from the African continent. Then they were illegally acquired. Forget mutiny. Forget piracy and murder and all the rest. The preeminent issue is the 'wrongful transfer of stolen goods.'" Baldwin shrugged. "Either way, we win."

Tappan could no longer listen quietly. "Sir, this is a moral issue. This war must be waged on the battlefield of righteousness."

Joadson stifled a groan.

"These are people, Mr. Baldwin. Not livestock. Did Christ hire a lawyer to get him off on technicalities? No. He went to the cross, sir. Nobly. And you know why? To make a statement—as we must."

Baldwin now seemed very much confused. He paused for a moment, studying the two men. "But Mr. Tappan," he said, "Christ *lost.* You—or at least you, Mr. Joadson—want to win, don't you? I certainly do. I sometimes don't get paid unless I do."

No one spoke for a long moment. Baldwin broke the strained silence with practical matters. "Speaking of pay— In order to do a better job than the lawyer who represented the Son of God, I'll require two and a half dollars a day."

◆ ◆ ◆

42

With Baldwin's departure, Joadson exchanged a long look with his fellow abolitionist. "You know, Mr. Tappan," he finally said, "the man might be right."

"You're saying that only because he's the last person on the list."

Joadson paused a second to consider. "Maybe so."

Inside, he prayed that the matter was as simple as Baldwin believed. But in an American court, nothing could be *that* simple.

12

In the prison courtyard, war was brewing.

Cinque and Buakei watched the townspeople streaming into the small building across the street from their prison. A bell clanged over the people's heads. A few people dressed all in black faced the prison on their knees, their heads bowed, their hands clasped together in front of them.

"Who are they, do you think?" asked Buakei.

"I don't know, but they look miserable." Cinque turned his attention to their own predicament. He looked around the prison courtyard and felt dismayed by what he saw.

They had separated themselves into tribal villages. The groups kept to their own kind. Mende men encamped on one side of the muddy courtyard. Temne warriors huddled around Yamba across the way.

The unity of their fight for freedom at sea seemed to have been forgotten. Their traditional rivalries now poisoned the air.

The Sherbro, the Kono, the Lokko, the Temne, the Mende ate their breakfast of steaming rice, each jealously guarding their sacred turf, suspiciously watching the others.

Cinque saw Fala, the lone Kissi, the strange one, fierce and unfriendly, unwelcome, off in a corner alone. He had no brothers to eat rice with. He had no rice to eat.

Cinque crossed the charged air of the courtyard and offered Fala a bowl of "Mende" rice.

He felt the others watch him with disdain.

"Perhaps Sengbe is brave," Yamba commented loudly, his voice full of sarcasm, calling Cinque by his true, African name. "Brave enough to get close to a flea-ridden Kissi."

"Stupid Mende," a Lokko man added.

"What did you say, you filthy Lokko potato eater?" Buakei challenged the man. The other cowered away. Buakei returned to his meal of rice and the frog he had caught in a mud puddle that morning.

Cinque ignored all of that. He attempted a friendly conversation with the Kissi man. "Why do you sharpen your teeth like sticks?" he carefully asked Fala, not wanting to offend.

Fala smiled and gestured Cinque closer, as if he had a secret no one else should hear.

"It's to impress the ladies," Fala said and smiled.

Cinque smiled, too, the first smile on his face for *months*. But the grin quickly dropped when Fala coughed up blood.

◆ ◆ ◆

That morning brought Baldwin, Joadson, and another man to the prison. Escorted by a guard, they sat at a table in the middle of the courtyard, not realizing they'd landed on Sherbro territory.

"How do you do?" Baldwin held out his hand to the first man who approached.

The man, a Sherbro, promptly moved the table to the edge of "Konoland" and drew a line in the mud with his foot.

Immediately, the Kono shoved the table to the Mende camp and marked their territory as well.

The boundaries were clear—the insult unmistakable. A Mende placed the table on Temne ground. This, all the Africans knew, meant trouble.

Yamba ordered the table removed to a far-off corner, up against a wall. His stare at Baldwin and the other visitors made it clear he was in charge. "You're a big man," he said in Temne to the well-dressed Joadson. "But not as big as me."

46

Joadson had no idea what Yamba had said, but he replied politely to the challenge.

Sensing the tension, though not understanding Yamba's words, Baldwin tried to make peace. He offered Yamba his hand. "I'm Roger Baldwin. This is Theodore Joadson, of the Anti-Slavery Society. And Professor Gibbs," he pointed to the third man, "a linguist."

"What do you want?" Yamba demanded in Temne.

Baldwin turned expectantly to Gibbs. But the professor shrugged his shoulders. He could not translate the words.

"Keep talking. Get them to talk," he advised.

From a sheath, Baldwin produced a heavy sword. It was one from the *Amistad*.

The men around the table stepped back, all except Yamba.

"Have you seen this before?" Baldwin asked.

Yamba continued to stare, menacing, his every look a threat.

Undaunted, Baldwin pushed on. "Where are you from?"

Gibbs repeated the question in Swahili.

The prisoners laughed.

"What did he say?" a Temne asked Yamba.

"It's gibberish," Yamba replied.

47

"What did he say?" Baldwin asked Gibbs.

"I think he said, 'Show me the map.'"

Happy to be making progress, Baldwin unfurled a parchment map and gestured to Yamba. "Is this where you're from?" he asked, pointing to Africa. "Or here?" Baldwin persisted, this time in Spanish. "The Caribbean? Were you born in the West Indies?"

"They are all idiots," Yamba proclaimed and stalked away.

Baldwin's shoulders drooped. "This is impossible." Was there no one there who could understand that he had come to help?

And then it happened. All that was needed was a word, a look, a shove, a spilled bowl of rice—Buakei and the Lokko man exchanging harsh words—and war broke out across the courtyard. Pushing, shoving, fists to flesh, then all-out melee as the tribes battled, taking out months of captivity on the ones who shared their terrible condition. Turning against each other.

◆ ◆ ◆

As their coach clattered away from the uproar at the prison, Roger Baldwin grumbled, "They're hopeless. You're hopeless, Professor. Well, fine! I will do it without their help!"

48

13

"I thought you took care of this annoying business!" President Van Buren exclaimed. He still had an election to win. He gave his secretary of state a stern look. Seated at his desk in the White House office, he held the letter "written" by the nine-year-old girl in a tiara.

"*As slave owning nations,*" the letter said, "*we must together stand firm. . . . The Africans must never go free.*"

Forsyth tried to explain. "We're in the process of . . . taking care of it." He sat down and dipped a quill into ink, waiting for Van Buren's dictated response.

Wearily, the president began. "Your Majesty—" He stopped to consider the absurdity. "I am speaking to a nine-year-old girl."

"If I were king of America, I could make this matter disappear. However, my hands are stayed by the Constitution of these United States." He stopped again, thinking of that document, wondering again about the wisdom of the words it contained, the messy business of shared power, the annoying Bill of Rights.

"Nevertheless," he concluded, "Her Majesty should expect her property to be delivered—"

◆　◆　◆

The next day, the little African girls clopped into the courtroom wearing American dresses and shoes. Looking even more uncomfortable in American clothes, the African men once again filed into the building.

Baldwin had watched them go into the courthouse, passing by missionaries who prayed for their souls. "God's blessing on you this morning," one had declared to the tall man, Yamba. The big prisoner had scowled and grabbed the bible from the other's hand. The missionary had not dared to ask for it back.

Once inside the courtroom, Baldwin's scrutiny remained mostly on Cinque. That one had said nothing to him during his prison visit. He had not participated in the fight either. He was the one who had actually killed the *Amistad* captain. But his face remained stoic and his eyes surveyed the room with intelligence. Perhaps he was a vicious killer, Baldwin thought, but he must also have been, at one time, a prince.

Cinque's face showed no emotion at all when Prosecutor Holabird waved the cane knives from the *Amistad* attack before the jury.

"I cannot overstate the inhumanity of their acts. The savagery. The blood lust—"

Holabird's words stirred the jury. But Baldwin knew the story was only half told. How could he communicate the Africans' version, when the men spoke no word of English and he, Baldwin, understood not one word of their language.

When Holabird concluded, Roger Baldwin stood up.

Disheveled as always, regarding the judge and jury over his wire-frame glasses, Baldwin began his defense. "This case isn't about murder or mayhem or massacres. It's about knowing the difference between here—and there."

Baldwin crossed to stand before Fala. "Open your mouth."

Fala glared at the attorney.

Baldwin repeated the command in Spanish. Still no movement from the Kissi.

"He doesn't understand. Stand up!" he said to a Mende man, again in English and Spanish.

Not one of the Africans moved.

"What is your name?" he asked another. "Is it José as Señor Ruiz claims? Are these men Cuban slaves, born on a plantation? Your Honor, these men are Africans. They don't belong to the queen of Spain anymore than you do."

"You have no proof!" Holabird exclaimed.

"And I have a bill of sale," Ruiz's lawyer piped in. "It shows that my client purchased these slaves in Havana. It lists their names: José, Bernardo, Paco—" He pointed out Fala, Yamba, and Buakei in turn. "They are Black Cubans, born as slaves."

"Show me a Cuban with teeth like this." Baldwin grabbed Fala's mouth and forced it open.

The entire courtroom gasped at the sight.

Judge Judson frowned from his place on the bench. "Yes, but Mr. Baldwin, do you have any documentation—any proof?"

Baldwin stood firmly before the court. "Your Honor, I have *them.*"

Judge Judson, long suffering over the entire matter, regarded the Africans with distaste.

◆ ◆ ◆

"I thought you did quite well," Joadson told Baldwin after court was dismissed for the day. They stood outside the courthouse.

52

"Well, thank you," Baldwin replied. The lawyer wasn't so sure. He needed something that would reveal the false claims of the Spaniards. Without documentation, how could he win his case?

The rattle of chains drew his attention to the courthouse steps, as the prisoners were led into the street.

Baldwin watched them, growing more and more wary as they came closer. The princely one stared at him with a look so intense, it frightened the lawyer. As they passed Baldwin and Joadson, that one spoke to Baldwin.

"Ngi kɔlɔ gbɔɔ bi longɔ binde."

His words meant nothing to Baldwin, but the urgency with which he spoke them was clear.

The neck chain jerked. The African prisoners moved on. Baldwin watched them disappear down the street before turning to Joadson. "What was that all about?" he said.

14

If he could just make him understand.

Guards led Cinque across the dark courtyard, his hands and ankles in manacles, the chains clanking with each step. The American, Baldwin, held out his hand. Cinque grasped it and pulled it to his chest. This was a Mende greeting, a warm and heartfelt welcome.

Cinque had listened to this man speaking in court, though he hadn't understood his words. But the man's gestures, his actions, made Cinque believe he understood what the man was trying to say. Cinque had tried to talk to him outside the courthouse as they were all being led back to the prison. Now, the young man stood before him. Perhaps he had understood.

The guards left them alone.

"I need to prove where you're from," the man said in English.

"You want to show them where we're from," Cinque said in Mende.

They regarded each other with mixed expressions of hope and despair. Neither one could break through the barrier that nationality and an ocean had erected between them.

"How are you to tell me?" Baldwin said.

"How can I explain?" Cinque wondered.

Moments of silence as the two men crouched together. Then Baldwin tapped the ground.

"This is my home." He drew a shape in the dirt. "Here."

Cinque looked. He understood.

"This is Cuba," Baldwin continued. He drew another, smaller shape, a boat and water. "This is where you—where everyone was killed. The *Amistad*."

Baldwin drew "Africa" about eighteen inches away from the small shape. "Is this your home? It is, isn't it? Isn't it!"

Cinque looked at this new shape, confused. What did that mean?

Frustrated, he stood and walked away. Baldwin just sat there. Another failure.

But then Cinque stopped. His muscular form

shone in the moonlight as he stood on a spot far across the courtyard. A long way from Baldwin's little drawing in the sand.

"Here!" he called out in his language. "Far, far away. This is *my home!*"

Baldwin grinned. Cinque nodded in response.

Finally—someone understood.

15

Joadson could not stand up straight. The ceiling was only four feet higher than the floor. The only light came from his flickering lantern, but he could see the horrible remnants—rusted ankle, hand, and neck manacles strewn about.

He shivered, and closed his eyes to steady his nerves.

The hull timbers of the *Amistad* creaked and groaned.

His own mother and father had come to America on a ship like this.

Joadson reached out and touched a dark stain—dried blood.

Then he saw a small trinket lodged between the timbers. He picked it up, a handmade figure on a thin leather string. Joadson held onto it tightly

57

because it meant something. It had meant a great deal to one of the Africans trapped in this dark, evil hold for months.

Suddenly, a loud bang and a cry of pain behind him! Joadson dropped the lamp and the whole place became as black as pitch. A chamber of horrors! Joadson cried out in panic, "Mr. Baldwin?"

"It's me." Baldwin's voice came out of the darkness. He must have stumbled coming down the steps.

"Light the lamp," Joadson said. He wanted to get out of there.

"I'm trying!" Joadson could hear him groping about the hold. Baldwin finally found his lantern and managed to relight it. "There. Are you all right?"

Joadson wasn't sure. He took several deep breaths. He found he was still clutching the trinket. "Yes," he finally answered.

Baldwin didn't appear to have found anything in the *Amistad*'s charts or navigational maps to disprove Ruiz's claims. Then, in the glowing light, Joadson followed Baldwin's gaze to something in the shadows . . . a leather pouch.

"What's this?" he asked.

◆　◆　◆

They were all back in court. This time, Baldwin spoke with an air of triumph. He held a sheaf of water-stained, tattered papers before the jury.

"At first glance perhaps, these papers appear to bolster the prosecution's case. They list cargo—cargo bearing the very Spanish names Misters Ruiz and Montes insist represent my clients."

He paused dramatically and rifled through the sheets.

"But—lo!" he exclaimed. "This is not the manifest of the *Amistad* at all. Look. This is part of the cargo manifest of a Portuguese vessel. The notorious transatlantic slave ship—the *Tecora*."

Sudden distress swept the prosecution's table. Montes glowered at Ruiz. Judge Judson directed a long, hard look at Holabird.

"Whatever these men say from this point on clearly matters not, Your Honor, because this proves them liars."

Baldwin set the papers before the judge.

"My clients' journey did not begin in Havana as these Spanish men claim. It began," he looked at Cinque, "much, *much* farther away.

"These men and women are not slaves, are not property, and never have been. They were kidnapped from their homes in Africa—rose up against their kidnappers as I dare say you or I would have if we had half their courage. And they sit before you now *still* in chains."

Baldwin concluded. "I have no doubt, Your Honor, that justice will prevail, that humanity will triumph."

◆ ◆ ◆

Baldwin smiled broadly in the hallway of the courthouse a few minutes later, confident that the judge and jury now could render no other verdict than complete freedom for Cinque and the others.

Tappan shook his hand. Joadson stood by proudly. Congratulations, it seemed, were in order.

Then suddenly, Baldwin felt a hard blow across the side of his head. Howling in pain, he turned in time to catch a glimpse of his assailant running away.

Joadson took off in pursuit but soon returned, winded and without his attacker. Baldwin exclaimed, "What did I do to deserve that?"

"You took this case, Mr. Baldwin," Joadson replied.

16

Huddled at the massive oaken desk in the presidential office, President Van Buren conspired with Secretary of State Forsyth and Presidential Aide Hammond.

"I wish someone would tell me what this means. You, yourself, Leder, said it was *meaningless.*"

Dourfaced, Hammond replied, "Not anymore, sir."

Forsyth explained the dilemma facing them. "If the Africans are executed, the abolitionists will gain sympathy for their cause. If, on the other hand, they are freed—the Southern states will rise against you. Then you can forget about being re-elected."

Van Buren groaned. "Over this?"

"It gets worse. In addition to inspiring uprisings in every state by American Negroes," Forsyth warned, "it could take us all one long step closer to civil war."

The president's eyes widened. He could not believe what he was hearing.

But it appeared to be true. Newspapers had spread the *Amistad* story to all parts of the country. In small towns and big cities, in the South and the North, people had lined up on one side or the other: "Free the Africans and let them go home!" or "Hang the murderous cannibals from the nearest tree!"

The division between pro-slavery and anti-slavery Americans had deepened over this now controversial case, Forsyth explained.

"But all is not lost," the secretary added. "It appears Judge Judson is going to free them. But . . ."

Van Buren looked up hopefully.

". . . judges can be replaced."

◆ ◆ ◆

Baldwin received the news in his office. Joadson was with him as he read the decree.

The lawyer crumpled the paper in disgust.

Just then, the farmer entered, this time without the goats, but instead leading a big pink pig into the room.

"Mr. Baldwin, you did it. We won!" the farmer

said. "I can't pay you money. But I want you to have my best sow."

Baldwin, still bursting with anger over the letter, ignored the farmer and the pig and hurled his desk lamp against a far wall. The pig squealed in terror and ran for cover. Baldwin picked up a crate of papers and sent it crashing after the lamp.

They had done it. The president and his cronies. They had snatched victory away, like pulling a rug from beneath their feet, sending Baldwin—and the Africans—tumbling.

Judge Judson had been replaced by another judge, handpicked by Secretary Forsyth. This one, Judge Coglin, no doubt would render a decision that the president, and the South, could live with.

◆ ◆ ◆

Adams's help was crucial. Joadson had ridden all night to Boston to stand before John Quincy Adams once more.

"If it were you trying the case—" he began.

"It isn't I," Adams said. "Thank God for that." He devoted his attention to the frail plant he had taken from the Capitol gardens.

"But if it were you, what would you do?"

Finally, Adams turned to face Joadson.

"When I was a young attorney," Adams said, "a

long time ago, I realized—after much trial and error—that in a courtroom, whoever tells the best story wins."

Joadson was unsure what the old man's words meant.

Adams went on. "What is their story? You and this so-called lawyer Baldwin have proven you know *what* they are; they are Africans. Congratulations." Sarcasm laced the ex-president's words. "Now, what you *don't* know, and as far as I can tell, haven't bothered in the least to find out, is *who* they are."

With that, Adams returned to his little plant. He made it clear: those were the last words he meant to say about the *Amistad* Africans.

17

Fala was dying.

He lay on the hard cot, shivering, coughing, trying to sleep. Cinque carried his only blanket toward Fala. But two Temne "guards" blocked his way.

"Give this to the Kissi."

One man pulled the blanket through the bars that separated them, but he gave it to Yamba—who now had two.

"Pass the blanket *on*," Cinque demanded.

"Be quiet," Yamba said. He held the bible he had taken from the missionary in his hand. "I'm trying to read."

Cinque banged on the bars, refusing to stop until Yamba relented. "All right, you ignorant shrieking Mende!" He threw the blanket on top of Fala.

65

Fala, in a weak voice, said, "Thank you."

Yamba turned back to Cinque. "You are not the 'big man' here. Don't forget that."

He went back to his "reading."

18

Baldwin could hear the commotion as he and Joadson entered the prison gates.

The Africans stood before the prison guards, all except Yamba and a few of his brothers, enraged, shouting in the face of loaded rifles pointed at them.

"What happened?" Baldwin asked a shaky prison guard.

"One of them died," he said. "We were taking the body out to bury it. And this happened. What do they want? Do they want to live with it?"

Baldwin and Joadson stared at the body lying stiff and cold on the ground. Baldwin turned to James Covey, the young British sailor they'd met the night before.

After a brief lesson from Professor Gibbs, who had taught Baldwin and Joadson to count to ten in Mende, the two men had spent the previous night combing the New Haven wharf in search of newly arrived Africans who might be able to translate Cinque's words. They'd gone from table to table in the smoky seaside tavern, counting to anyone who would listen. Finally, they had caught the attention of a young sailor who had been conversing with his mates at a crowded table. The young man, James Covey, was a British sailor, but he was also a Mende African who had been captured by Spanish slave traders and rescued by the British Navy when he was just a boy. Now, at nineteen, he was a man who spoke both English and Mende fluently.

After Baldwin and Joadson explained the Africans' dilemma, Covey had agreed to join their defense team at once.

"They want to bury him," Covey now told the Americans as they faced the angry crowd in the courtyard. "They have to bury him according to their *poro* beliefs."

Baldwin and Joadson exchanged a pleased look over Covey's head. Already Covey had proved his usefulness. Because of him they had, maybe, a chance of winning their case.

◆ ◆ ◆

Fala's body would be buried in an American cemetery, but he would have a *poro* burial. Cinque had been chosen by the others—over Yamba—to perform the official ceremony. Inside the prison cell, the elders washed Fala's body with rags heated over a small fire. Carefully, with reverence, Cinque marked Fala's hand with a sharpened stick.

"There. You'll be recognized when you return."

Then he wrapped the body in a cloth.

The solemn group of Africans chanted in Mende, in Temne, in Sherbro, in Kono, in Lokko around the ragged grave. The three little girls fell to the ground wailing, rubbing mud over their faces, and unbraiding their hair.

"The unexpected always happens. We did what we could, but our efforts were in vain. The proud warrior Fala is dead," Cinque said. They lowered Fala's body into the ground. Then Cinque draped his blanket—his only blanket—over it.

The other men laid branches over the corpse as they sang a Mende funeral chant:

Fala, Fala, be accepted in the paradise of the creator.
Yes, Fala, we pray, be accepted in a blanket in Heaven.

Then each took a handful of dirt and dropped it into the grave. Cinque watched as the new man, clearly an African but one who wore a sailor's uniform, broke from the group of Americans to join the

69

Africans around the grave. The Americans stood some distance away, but in their respectful silence, Cinque thought that perhaps they, too, understood the importance of sending a soul on its journey.

"Fala, we built you a house—this grave. But we can't provide you with any money. We haven't any. I apologize," Cinque said.

With those final words to Fala, he stepped back. The funeral was over. But Cinque wondered as he trudged back to the jail, how many more of them would die in this cold place before they returned to their home.

♦ ♦ ♦

Later that night in his prison cell, Cinque sat facing the odd Ensign Covey. He spoke Mende, but he spoke English as well. He looked African, but he wore British clothes.

Could he be trusted?

Baldwin and Joadson waited silently as Covey and Cinque talked.

"My name is Kai Nyagua—and James Covey. I was rescued off a slave ship by the British Navy. I never went back." The young man turned to indicate Baldwin. "You and he will talk to each other through me," he said to Cinque. Then he nodded to Baldwin, who took a deep breath and began to explain.

"A problem has arisen," he said. "The judge we had who believed you should be freed has been replaced."

"How is that possible?" Cinque wanted to know. "Chiefs can't be replaced." In Cinque's Mani village, once a man reached such a high honor, it was his for life—even after death.

"It doesn't make sense to you, or to me. I can't explain it. Only, it has happened."

Baldwin stopped to think a minute, then went on. "I need you to help me," he admitted. "When we return to court, I need you to speak."

Cinque drew back and shook his head. "I am not an advisor of any kind. I certainly can't speak for the others."

"They say you can. They say you're the 'big man' here."

Cinque shook his head again.

"They say you alone—*alone*—slew the most terrifying beast anyone had ever seen, the lion. It's not true?"

Cinque sighed. Buakei had no doubt told the story. Now he had to explain about the lion.

"It had killed several people in our village," he began slowly. "Everyone, including me, was afraid. Even the warriors."

He closed his eyes, remembering, picturing the

71

terrifying scene when, one night as he slept with his family, the lion appeared out of nowhere, hungry, vicious, ready to kill again.

Cinque had no weapon nearby. Only a rock. He lured the beast away from his sleeping wife and children and threw the rock with all his strength.

"And by some miracle, I hit it. I don't know how that killed it, but it did."

He couldn't believe it then; he couldn't believe it now.

"Everyone praised me. They gave me lots of land. They gave me respect. And I took it all, even though I didn't deserve any of it. It was an accident. I was lucky. If I had missed . . . ? No one would be telling you about it now. I'd just be dead."

He looked at Baldwin, wanted this man to understand. He was just a man, like any other, protecting his family.

"I'm not a 'big man,'" Cinque said.

Baldwin thought a long moment before he replied. "I might agree with you. Except for one thing. The *other* lion—the *Amistad.* That, too, was an accident?"

Cinque shrugged. "That wasn't bravery. Any man would do the same to get back to his family. You would do it."

They watched each other in the flickering lamplight. Baldwin, after a moment, nodded. But would he have had the courage?

He looked to Joadson, and Joadson immediately understood. He handed the small charm he had found in the *Amistad*'s slave hold over to Baldwin.

"Someone said this is yours?"

For the first time, Cinque looked ready to break down. He delicately took the small charm from Baldwin and turned it over and over in his hands.

"My wife gave this to me," he explained. "To keep me safe."

No one spoke for a long time. Then Baldwin said softly, "I want you to tell me how you got here. From so far away. Tell us your story."

19

Although he sat in his prison cell talking to Baldwin and Joadson, Cinque traveled back in his mind to his Mani village in Sierra Leone. He pictured his vast fields of rich black soil, ripe for growing rice and cassandra. He looked up into the sky that arched like a dome over his head. He gazed out past the fields to the lush jungle beyond. He smelled rain in the air.

"My brother-in-law Bato warned that the rain would never come. He worried about our farm. No rain, no crops, no money—we would all starve.

"'It'll rain,' I assured him. But he doubted me still, looking up and seeing no clouds, nothing but bright blue sky and brilliant yellow sun.

"'Finish the planting,' I told him.

"'What's the use?'

"'It'll rain,' I said once more, then cracked

knuckles with him and turned to go. He was younger than I, and sometimes foolish. I was the oldest son of my father. It was my responsibility to make sure the planting was done.

"I left him in the rice fields to return to the village. I had departed so early that morning, my wife and three children were still sleeping. Now, they would be awake. We could take a meal together. Then I would return to work.

"I walked the familiar, mile-long path, lined on both sides by the lush jungle. I loved this walk. Before me, I could see the village in the distance. People were up and about. My father's hut lay in the center, all the others surrounding him. He was the big man in Mani. Old and feeble, but with a mind as sharp as a spear.

"As I walked, I felt something small touch the top of my head. I stopped, held my hand out. Another drop. *Rain!* I smiled to myself. The gods were good.

"I could see my wife emerge from our house, my young son trailing behind her, playful as a cub. With a light heart, I made my way down the path.

"Suddenly, someone grabbed me from behind and yanked me to the ground. I knew immediately what this meant. A coarse net—used to trap animals—fell around me as three Vey tribesmen held me down. I recognized the men. They had been sent by Birmaja, a prince in a nearby village to whom I owed a debt.

I pleaded with them. One more rice planting, I explained, and I would pay all that I owed. But they shoved me to the ground and ignored my plea. I began to scream out to Bato, to the workers, to the people I could see in my distant village. I thrashed about in their grasp, knowing I had to fight with all my strength. If I didn't, if these men took me away—I knew where I was headed. It had happened to some of our villagers before.

"'Bato!' I yelled. But he was too far away. A rope bound my hands, a gun pointed at my head. 'Tafe!' I wailed in despair as they forced me into the jungle. The last thing I saw was my wife and son—so far away.

"For days and nights, we marched. I had an iron collar clamped around my neck. Along the way, we met up with other kidnappers and their captives. I saw one I knew.

"'Sengbe,' Buakei said. Nothing more was spoken. Dejected and wishing for death rather than what lay ahead of us, we were forced on. The rain poured relentlessly.

"Finally, we reached the high iron gate of Lomboko, the slave factory we had all heard about in our villages.

"Hundreds of men, women, and children locked together like animals waiting for slaughter in a

76

holding pen. Some had fallen sick. Already, many had died. But hundreds remained, human cargo that the white man, in his white clothes and white hat, sold to the other men for coins of gold.

"I resisted. I tried to bargain for my release, but my offers moved no one. I fought back, refused to accept their enslavement. But I was beaten and punished. I cried—yes, I cried—and prayed for death.

"But none of it worked. Like one moving, miserable field of black bodies, we were forced aboard a great ship, larger than the *poro* meeting room in Mani. I stood in awe of the size of this boat, with its crisp white sails and hanging ropes. I looked about me as more and more men, women, children were led on board and herded toward a small, dark opening that even from a distance reeked from the smell of too many bodies crowded together. The terror of what lay before me, before us all, beyond that door, down in that hold, across the waters to who knew where, drove me to fight against it. With all my strength, I resisted being thrust down into that slave hold, but the guards were many and they had weapons. As they shoved me into the foul-smelling hold, I turned to get one last glimpse of the jewel-green shore of Africa and the blazing sun, rising in glory over Mendeland.

"On days when the ship sailed on calm waters, our voyage down below was horrible. People screamed in agony, cried out in pain. On days and nights when the storms rocked the boat in violent swells, people fell upon each other, crushing those beneath.

"Every day and every night, people sickened and died. I saw a young mother, ailing and afraid, clutch her two small children in frail arms.

"We had to throw the dead ones overboard where sharks swam in hungry anticipation. I myself, I was assigned this gruesome task. I watched the sharks tear a lifeless body to shreds in less than a minute.

"Every day, there was a little more room in the slave deck. But there was never enough food, never enough water. We all grew weak, but some—the very old, the very young, those who were weak beforehand—grew more and more wretched. The sick mother had only one child left, a little girl. The other child had died of starvation and bloody flux. Then, one day, as I worked cleaning filth from the deck, I looked across and saw her. The mother looked at me, her eyes wild with despair, the child's eyes white with terror. In a second, before my own helpless sight, she leaped—with her child crushed in her arms—over the side of the ship and into the water, into the jaws of the ravenous sharks.

"Another day, while the 'healthy' ones worked on deck, the Spanish sailors dragged a huge fishing net across the floor. It was filled with heavy cannon

78

balls, big as coconuts. Why? I wondered as I watched the sailors, curious at first, and then with growing horror as they tied fifty or more sick Africans to the weighted net.

"My stomach turned over many times. I realized what they meant to do. *Everyone* realized what they meant to do.

"I fought to try to save them. But how could I? The heavy chains weighed my every move, the wide, unfamiliar seas every day took me further away from everything I knew and understood. The sharks trailed alongside the boat, waiting, waiting, hungry and waiting.

"I stood helpless as the Spanish sailors kicked the net—and all fifty people—overboard."

◆ ◆ ◆

Baldwin, Joadson, and even Covey listened in silence as Cinque told his story of the Middle Passage from Africa across the Atlantic to Cuba.

The next day in court, Cinque told it again—to a room full of white and black spectators who seemed to stop breathing, so stunned were they by the horror of his tale.

Cinque spoke without hesitation, though his voice was choked at times and at other times, sharp with indignation.

79

Baldwin stood before him in the courtroom. Covey sat next to the witness chair, faithfully translating the harsh words.

"Finally, after months over rough waters, we reached land. Many white people there, more than I had imagined existed in the world. All so busy, trading papers for coins, coins for clothes, clothes for rum, and all of it for slaves. Others—not quite white, not quite black—an unsightly mixture of the two, but slaves anyway, hurried about doing the white men's bidding. They led us to another slave prison, this one even larger than the one we'd left at Lomboko. Here, they fed us rice and ripe bananas—all that we could eat. To fatten us up for what we feared would be our last meal. We still worried that the white men meant to cut us up and roast us, like the cook on the ship had said.

"They made us dance, do acrobatics, and rub rich oil over our bodies so our black skins would glisten like gold. I realized very soon that we were not meant to be food, but to be sold."

Here, Cinque paused. And despite his Mende training and *poro* values, he hung his head before this crowded room as shame laced his words. "They put us on display like we were nothing more than beasts, prodded and inspected. Naked, exposed—even the women—wearing nothing but manacles, leg irons, and chains."

They were sold, Cinque said, to Ruiz and Montes. Fifty-three of them—forty-nine men and four children. They were once again loaded onto a ship, this one smaller and sleeker—the *Amistad*. They were to be taken to a sugar plantation, where they would be worked all the day long in the hot sun.

Cinque told the court about the loose nail and their fierce fight for freedom. "I wanted to kill them, too," he said, pointing to Ruiz and Montes. "But they convinced some of us that they would take us back home."

Of course, all now knew they had lied.

Baldwin stepped away from his witness and returned to his seat. No one, not even the new judge, could manage to speak for several moments. Then, Judge Coglin signaled to Holabird, who rose and faced Cinque with a sardonic smile.

"Quite a tale," Holabird said, making it clear he believed not a word of it.

"Isn't it true," Holabird said, "that certain African tribes, for hundreds—perhaps thousands—of years, have owned slaves?"

Cinque answered uneasily. "Yes."

Holabird said, "I see."

James Covey interrupted. "I don't think you do 'see.'"

"Who asked you?" Holabird protested.

"It's different," Covey continued.

The judge warned the young man to be silent, but Covey could not hold his tongue.

"The Mende word for 'slave,' in fact, is 'worker—'"

Holabird roared over Covey's words. "Do these 'workers' receive wages? Are they free not to work? Your Honor, the translator is answering for the witness!"

"The witness is not being given a chance to answer," Baldwin shouted his objection.

Holabird kept talking, over Baldwin, over the judge, over Covey, over Cinque. "Whatever you want to call it, the concept is the same. It's all about money, isn't it? Slaves—production—money! That's the idea of it. Whether it's here or there!"

He turned on Cinque and spoke so rapidly, Covey could not translate it quickly enough. "Why would the Spanish men kill their own slaves," he demanded, "when slaves mean money?

"The behavior you attribute to your tormenters—your victims—and therefore everything else you've said makes no sense. But thank you for it. Like all good *works of fiction,* it was entertaining."

He turned on his heels and stalked away. Cinque, confused, lost in all the words, watched Holabird, his heart sinking lower and lower.

20

His head pounding, Cinque returned to his seat. The sad images of his trip on the *Tecora* still troubled his sight. He felt lower than he had for a long time, if that were possible.

His story was true, every word. But maybe they didn't believe him. He could not tell because he could not understand what they were saying. Maybe the young Mende/British man had not said it the right way. Maybe, *he—Cinque*—had failed.

◆ ◆ ◆

Baldwin now called his second witness of the day. He called Captain Fitzgerald, a British naval officer who knew about the slave factory, though he had never been able to find it—it was hidden so well. Fitzgerald knew about the slave ship *Tecora,* of such horrors as Cinque had described.

"Often when slavers are intercepted or believe they might be, they simply throw all the prisoners overboard—and thereby rid themselves of the evidence of their crime," Fitzgerald testified.

"If only we could corroborate Cinque's story, with evidence of some kind," said Baldwin. He pulled out the sheaf of papers he had found on the *Amistad*. He pretended he did not know what the *Tecora* papers—the ones Ruiz and Montes had tried unsuccessfully to conceal—had to say.

"If you look," said Fitzgerald, "there's a notation made on May tenth—'correcting' the number of slaves on board, reducing their number by fifty. I'd say that means that the *Tecora* crew, having underestimated the provisions required for the journey, solved the problem by throwing fifty people overboard."

◆ ◆ ◆

Cinque could not pay attention to the witness, nor did he listen to Ensign Covey's translation. His mind was elsewhere. His wife—he wanted to be home with Tafe. He missed her terribly at that moment. His children, so young. What must they think about their father? Would they understand? Would they think he had abandoned them? His father, so old. Was he still alive?

Homesickness washed over him like a tidal wave. It blotted out Baldwin's words, Holabird's words, the story Captain Fitzgerald was telling. His head pounded. A pen rolled to the floor. His head pounded. Yamba turned a page of his book. His head pounded. The American flag flapped in the wind just outside the courthouse window.

In the next moment, Cinque rose to his feet, calling out loudly in English, "Give us free!"

Everyone in the courtroom turned to look at him. Time seemed to stand still. Startled, then outraged, Holabird said to the judge, "Your Honor, please instruct the defendant that he cannot disrupt these proceedings with such—"

"Give us free!"

Baldwin looked over at Covey. Had he taught Cinque these words? Covey sat with a blank expression on his face.

"GIVE US FREE!"

Judge Coglin seemed too stunned to speak. Holabird seemed apoplectic. "He cannot keep screaming, 'Give us free'—or anything else—while I am trying to question this witness—"

"Give us free," Cinque said once more, in little more than a whisper, before he calmly sat down.

21

"You don't have to pretend to be interested in that. Nobody's watching but me."

For several minutes Cinque had watched Yamba flipping the pages of his bible in the dim light of the prison. Other than Yamba and Cinque, and Buakei and Maseray whispering through the bars, everyone was asleep.

Yamba glanced up. "I'm not pretending. I'm beginning to understand it."

He motioned Cinque to his side, then began to point out the pictures he had "read."

"Their people have suffered more than ours." He showed Cinque pictures of wars, beheadings, the burning of cities. "Then he was born and everything changed."

They had reached the picture of a baby, his mother bending over the manger, a star shining in the sky.

"Who is he?" Cinque asked.

"I don't know," said Yamba, "but everywhere he goes, he is followed by the sun."

More pictures—of a man healing the sick, welcoming the children, walking on water, always with a halo of light around his head.

Yamba turned more pages. "But then something happened. He was captured, accused of some crime. Here he is with his hands tied."

"He must have done something bad," Cinque said.

"Why?" Yamba said. "What did we do?"

He continued. "Whatever it was, it was serious enough to kill him for it. Do you want to see *how* they killed him? You've never seen anything like this—"

Cinque was troubled by the picture of the man and the two others each nailed to two crossed pieces of wood. Still he said, "These are just pictures, Yamba. This is just a story in a book."

But that was not the end of it. Yamba went on. "His people took his body down from this . . . this . . . this . . ." Yamba knew no word for it. He traced the outline of the crossed wood with his hands. "They wrapped him in a cloth, just like we do. They put him in a cave. They thought he was dead, but he appeared before his people again. He spoke to them. And, finally, he rose to the sky."

◆ ◆ ◆

87

President Van Buren wrote an order in his White House study. It was addressed to Lt. John S. Paine, of the U.S. Navy brig *Grampus*. It said he was to proceed immediately to the New Haven harbor. Upon the conclusion of the present trial—Van Buren had been assured Judge Coglin would decide his way—Lt. Paine was to pick up the slaves now imprisoned in that city, and transport them without delay to Cuba.

The president had to be sure. The election was only a few months away. He wanted the Africans found guilty of murder and sent on their way to Havana as quickly as possible. And whatever would happen to them there, so be it.

He had an election to win.

◆ ◆ ◆

"They will kill us, you know," Yamba said to Cinque, an unusual sense of peace in the Temne warrior's words. "This is where the soul goes when you die here." He pointed to another picture, the man in the heavens, bathed in light.

"It doesn't look so bad," Yamba said.

◆ ◆ ◆

Across town, a figure knelt in a Catholic church, silently praying at the altar before a statue of Christ.

It was Judge Coglin.

22

The huge masts of the warship *Grampus* towered over the New Haven rooftops as it pulled into the harbor the next morning. The massive foremast, followed by its even larger main and aft masts, looked exactly, as Yamba stared at them on his way to court, like the crossed pieces of wood erected to kill the men in his book.

Quietly, Yamba prayed.

◆ ◆ ◆

This time, everyone stood when the judge entered the courtroom, even Cinque, Baldwin noted. On this day, Judge Coglin would announce his verdict. In his heart, Baldwin was prepared for the worst. He had seen the *Grampus* moored in the harbor and suspected that arrangements had already been made to carry the prisoners back to Spain. The room waited silently for Coglin to begin.

"I find it impossible to deny the power of the government's position," Coglin said.

Forsyth, who had watched Coglin intently, let out a long breath. He seemed relieved and assured that the judge would do as the president had commanded.

Seeing satisfaction on Forsyth's face, Baldwin closed his eyes.

"However . . ." Coglin said, and Baldwin's eyes flew open. Forsyth stopped in midbreath. "I also believe Señors Ruiz and Montes may have misrepresented the origin of the prisoners. Were they born in Africa?"

Coglin repeated the question, making it clear to everyone that this was the fundamental issue before his court.

He studied the prisoners. Finally, he spoke. "Yes, I believe they were."

Eyes widened and mouths dropped open. Both sides were surprised by these words.

"As such, Her Majesty's claims of ownership have no merit—"

People began to shout.

"Neither do those for salvage made by Lieutenants Meade and Gedney."

More noise—protest and prayers.

Freedom is in sight, after a rebellion on *La Amistad.*

Cinque argues with Yamba about the fate of the Spaniards, Montes and Ruiz.

Maseray and the children are placed in a separate cell across the courtyard from the men.

The Africans are chained together and marched through the streets of New Haven on their way to the courthouse.

A prisoner once again, Cinque watches the iron doors slam shut.

Roger S. Baldwin offers his hand, but instead of shaking it, Cinque grasps it firmly and pulls it to his chest.

Abolitionist Theodore Joadson will do all he can to secure freedom for the Africans.

Baldwin holds up water-stained documents listing the human "cargo" of the notorious slave ship *Tecora*.

Cinque leads a prison riot, demanding to bury Fala according to the traditions of their homeland.

A mother in the slave hold cries out for her dying child, as described by Cinque on the witness stand.

John Quincy Adams sees for himself the humanity and dignity of Cinque as he examines a plant from home.

Cinque suddenly interrupts the court and shouts loudly, in English, "Give us free!"

Cinque stands at the bow of the merchant ship, sailing toward Africa, and freedom.

"I hereby order the immediate arrest of Señors Ruiz and Montes on the charge of slave trading."

Coglin now had to shout over the din.

". . . the release of the Africans and their conveyance by the government *back to their homes in Africa.*"

He banged his mallet for order. Baldwin leapt out of his seat and embraced the startled Joadson. He pointed to Cinque and shouted to Covey, "Tell him!"

Before Covey could translate, however, Cinque smiled. He understood. They were finally, once again, free.

◆ ◆ ◆

Celebrations in the prison courtyard included the Africans and three missionaries. The tribesmen, no longer separated in their encampments, chanted and sang songs of joy and praise. The black-clad Americans moved among them with their picture books in hand, ones like the one Yamba had shown to Cinque. A bonfire raged in the center of it all.

"We're here to teach you about the Savior, Jesus Christ of Nazareth," the apostles said to Cinque. Covey began to translate.

But Cinque walked right past them. He had other business on his mind.

91

"We have to talk," he said to Yamba.

"You should listen to them. My prayers to their god are what saved us," Yamba instructed.

The missionaries approached Cinque again. He tried to wave them off, but they persisted. "Your brother has accepted the Lord in his heart."

"*Kai!*" Cinque shouted past them. "I need them to be quiet. Make them understand." To Yamba he said, "Buakei wants to marry Maseray. We need your permission!"

For the first time since they'd met, the big Temne warrior looked completely surprised by Cinque's words. "That's impossible," he replied and walked away.

The forlorn look on Buakei's face forced Cinque to follow after Yamba, pushing his way past the persistent missionaries. "Yamba," Cinque implored, "we have to talk about this."

◆ ◆ ◆

All celebrating had ended in the hearts of Roger Baldwin, Theodore Joadson, and Lewis Tappan. Their carriage ride to the prison that night was as somber as a ride to a funeral. Once at the gate, Baldwin went in immediately. Best to get this grim task over with.

Joadson and Tappan remained in the carriage.

92

"Of course, this is bad news," Tappan was saying, "but the truth is, they may be more valuable to our struggle in death than in life."

Joadson looked for a long moment at his fellow abolitionist. Could he have heard what he thought he had heard?

"Martyrdom, Mr. Joadson. From the dawn of Christianity, we have seen no stronger power for change. You know it's true."

Joadson moved to get out of his seat. "What's true," he said to Tappan, "is that there are some men whose hatred of slavery is stronger than anything else. Except for their hatred of the slaves themselves."

"Allow me to open the door for you, sir." Joadson offered up his hand, like a good servant to his master. Tappan refused to take it.

Joadson walked away.

◆ ◆ ◆

Baldwin found Cinque and Yamba in deep conversation about Buakei's proposal and Maseray's desires.

"A great summit is in progress," Covey said cheerfully.

"Well, break it up. I have to talk to Cinque."

◆ ◆ ◆

93

The bonfire flamed and crackled, illuminating Baldwin's drawn face and downcast eyes. He watched Cinque across the small table placed in the center of the courtyard. Joadson stood nearby, and Covey sat ready to translate. Slowly, Baldwin began to speak.

"Our president, our 'big man,' has appealed the decision to the Supreme Court."

"What does that mean?" Cinque asked.

Baldwin sighed. "It means—we have to try the case again."

Cinque, once again, frowned in confusion. "You said there would be a judgment. And if we won the judgment, we'd go free."

"No, what I said—" Baldwin began to disagree.

Cinque interrupted. "*That's* what you said."

"No, what I said—"

"No!" Cinque shouted.

Baldwin stopped, trying to remember. Maybe he had said it. Certainly he had thought it. He understood why Cinque was having a hard time with this news.

"What I should have said," Baldwin began trying to explain.

But Covey broke in. "There is no Mende word for 'should.' You either do something or you don't."

The lawyer stared at them both. What could he say? "What I meant was—"

94

Covey shook his head.

"What I said to you before, about the judgment—" Baldwin tried once more, "is *almost* the way it works here."

Covey translated the word.

"Almost?" Cinque asked, staring at Baldwin.

Baldwin nodded, glad to be getting through.

"Almost," Cinque turned to Covey. He had what was *almost* a grin on his face, but it turned out to be more of a grimace. Cinque angrily overturned the table and yelled at the attorney.

"What kind of a place is this? Where you *almost* mean what you say? Where laws *almost* work? How can you live like that?"

Cinque pushed Baldwin aside, frustration spilling out of every pore. How could they *almost* be free? Why did people keep promising him things and going back on those promises?

He paced the yard before the fire, chanting louder and louder. The flames crackled as his outcries increased, the two sounds meshing into the clamor of a lion's roar.

23

Later that night, the prison courtyard was deserted, the fire reduced to glowing embers and wisps of smoke. Cinque lay in his prison cell, pretending to be asleep.

In his hand he cradled another spike. In his heart he harbored another insurrection. His allies this time included not only the other Africans (all except Yamba), but also the free black abolitionists of New Haven—led by the man who once had been a slave . . . Joadson.

Cinque broke the locks on their prison cells and the Africans escaped into the courtyard under cover of night. Yamba remained behind, reading his bible, praying to God, refusing—this time—to take part in Cinque's bloody battle for freedom. Yamba said he had found his freedom another way.

But not Cinque. Too long he had lingered in

the American prison. He'd put too much trust in American laws. It was time once again for the Africans to seize their own freedom, and to kill anyone who stood in their way.

◆ ◆ ◆

For months, Roger Baldwin had prepared for this case. He'd done everything well. He'd won. Now, he felt as disappointed as anyone, even Cinque. But he was also a man of the law, and he didn't like the look in Cinque's eyes when he'd left him that night.

Baldwin feared that the Africans, led by Cinque, might take matters into their own hands. He sent word to Colonel Pendleton through Bomoseen, the Abnaki Indian who prowled the wharf. "Meet me outside," the note read.

"I don't know for sure, but it's possible Cinque will try to escape," he told the colonel.

On receiving this news, Pendleton rushed to call up the local militia, rousing men from their beds, loading them onto two wagons with muskets at the ready.

They raced through the night to get back to the jail.

◆ ◆ ◆

Cinque picked at the lock of the prison's main gate. The others hovered around him. They heard horses' hooves pounding the ground in the distance. Joadson and the abolitionists, Cinque thought, were bringing wagons loaded with enough supplies to get them all to a place called Canada, a place with no slaves. He was expecting them. They were part of the plan.

The lock snapped, and Cinque pulled open the wooden gates. They swung wide and revealed—two rows of New Haven soldiers, down on their knees, their muskets dead-aiming at him and the other newly sprung prisoners.

Cinque looked along the line of white faces and settled on one, Roger Baldwin.

Baldwin stared back at Cinque, only at Cinque.

◆ ◆ ◆

Cinque was removed to a jail cell apart from all of his African brothers. This was his worst confinement yet. He paced his cell without rest, his fury not subsiding. He was angry at Baldwin, who had turned against him. He was angry at the fat jailor who had brought a new crop of spectators to see the beasts in their cages. Mostly, though, he was angry at himself, for failing *again.*

◆ ◆ ◆

98

"Where did he think he was going to go?" asked Baldwin later. He and Joadson sat at a table in the tavern. "How many people was he prepared to kill? How many of his own people were prepared to die?"

Joadson didn't answer. The lawyer was drunk, and Joadson didn't like that. He stared off into the distance at the ominous *Grampus* still anchored in the harbor, waiting, waiting. . . .

Baldwin grew visibly annoyed with Joadson's silence, which he read as the rebuke it was intended to be. "I suppose you would've helped them get away. All right, why didn't you?"

Refusing to reply, Joadson continued to look away.

"I suppose you think I should have, rather than—" Baldwin broke off.

Joadson turned to him now and finished the sentence. "Rather than betray him? You're right, that is what I think. It's also what you think."

For a while, they said nothing more, but the sudden tension between them made them both uncomfortable.

Baldwin finished his drink.

Joadson rose to leave.

"Since you obviously know everything," Baldwin said, his words twisted with bitterness, "tell me, *Mr.* Joadson. In which should we place our trust? Laws? Or lawlessness?"

"When our laws apply equally to us both, Mr. Baldwin, ask me again. If you're not too drunk to do so."

Joadson walked away, a disappointed, disillusioned man. First Tappan had revealed his true stripes. Now Baldwin.

The lawyer shouted after him, "Maybe you'd prefer those laws in a village somewhere in Sierra Leone. Or wherever you're from!" Joadson hoped Baldwin would regret those words.

◆ ◆ ◆

From somewhere nearby, perhaps from their new quarters in the jailor's own house, came the sound of the little African girls singing an American church song.

The girls' voices carried through the night. They reached Cinque as he paced his cell, inspiring his own chant in reply.

"A MU MA BATE . . ."

His chant echoed against the walls of his cramped isolation cell. Soon he heard Buakei's chant quietly join with his.

Two more Mende chimed in. Then others from all the tribes until their voices drowned out the American hymn.

All of them now, Yamba even, joined in one unified proclamation:

"Today is the day
We call on all our ancestors.
We are ready to face any situation.
Aa aa a mu ma bate!"

◆　◆　◆

Roger Baldwin, isolated in his own cell, his office, heard nothing more than the scratching of his quill against rough paper.

He wrote furiously, not wanting to stop for fear he would lose his nerve. It was a letter, addressed to: His Excellency, the Massachusetts member of the House of Representatives, John Quincy Adams.

"Sir, we need you," the letter read. "If ever there was a time for a man to cast aside his daily trappings and array himself for battle, that time has come.

"Cicero once said, appealing to Claudius in defense of the Republic, 'that the whole result of this entire war depends on the life of one most brave and excellent man.' In our time, in this instance, I believe it depends on two: a courageous man at present in irons in New Haven named Cinque . . . and you, sir."

Immediately upon signing it, Baldwin sent his appeal by courier to Adams's country home outside Boston.

♦ ♦ ♦

Adams received the letter the next morning, as he nursed his one sickly little plant in his greenhouse. He read it briefly, pondered its contents for a moment, then crumpled the paper and let it fall to the floor.

24

Roger Baldwin sat in his once crowded law office. Only one client, and the pig, remained.

Covey came in, stamping snow off of his shoes. He went to the fire in the hearth. Seeing Covey, Baldwin interrupted his meeting. "What did Cinque say?" he asked immediately.

Covey blew on his hands and held them before the fire. "He won't see you."

"He won't *see* me?" said Baldwin, incredulous and angry all at once. He reached for his coat. "I want to talk to him. Let's go."

Covey shook his head. "I have to respect his wishes."

Now Baldwin was truly furious. At all of them—Cinque, Joadson, Covey. He ordered the young British sailor out of his office and took off for the jail alone. "No, you stay," he said to the pig before he slammed the office door.

◆ ◆ ◆

When Baldwin arrived at the prison, Cinque refused to look at him, refused even to acknowledge his presence. Baldwin refused to leave.

"Has it occurred to you that I'm all you've got?"

Cinque said nothing, just sat in the cell holding the wooden charm in his large hands.

"Well, since my practice has deteriorated to virtually nothing, you're all I've got."

Baldwin opened his briefcase and pulled out a voodoo doll stuck with pins. "This is me." He next took out a noose made of twine. "This is for me. I've had death threats—some of them signed by my own clients. I should say, my former clients."

Still no reaction from Cinque.

Baldwin shrugged his shoulders and settled in. "I'm free to sit here as long as it takes for you to acknowledge me. You understand that word, don't you? 'Free.'"

Baldwin couldn't curb his tendency to be sarcastic. But Cinque didn't take the bait.

They sat there in silence, until a voice beyond the bars spoke. "Caesar," it said.

104

Baldwin turned with a start and nearly fell out of his chair. He could not believe the sight his own eyes presented.

"Cicero's appeal was to Julius Caesar—not Claudius. Claudius would not be born for another hundred years," said Old Man Eloquent.

Cinque regarded the ex-president with no interest. Adams returned the look. "Is that he?" he asked Baldwin.

"Yes, sir," Baldwin managed, still dumbfounded.

Adams turned to the guard and ordered him to unlock the door.

So John Quincy Adams was now on the case.

◆ ◆ ◆

Cinque recognized the power in the old man even before he learned of the position Adams had once held, the "big man" of all America. There was something in his ancient eyes, in his calm but commanding voice, in the way others bowed to that command. Baldwin, even that traitor, looked humble in the old man's presence. Adams had an effect on people, even on Cinque. Dare he hope, once more, that this meant one day he and the others would be free to return to their homes?

◆ ◆ ◆

Over the next weeks, Adams and Baldwin buried themselves in law books all day and all through the night. In Adams's book-lined study, lit by flaming gas lamps and a healthy fire, they barely stopped to eat or sleep. They spoke very little to each other, and then only about the *Amistad* case. They were running out of time. The Supreme Court would soon meet to hear their case.

Cinque knew the two men—one young and perhaps foolish, the other older and no doubt as wise as his own father—were somewhere far away working on his case. He wanted to help, to be involved in winning their freedom rather than just sitting on the sidelines, watching and waiting. He sent Covey back and forth from his jail cell to Adams's study with questions about the case.

"Does the American government have any treaties with West Africa?" Covey asked tentatively on this, his third trip to interrupt Adams's intense concentration on his law books.

"No," Adams gruffly replied.

"Cinque wants to know, does Spain have any treaties with West Africa?"

His patience paper thin, Adams replied, "No."

"Does the commonwealth of Connecticut have any treaties with—"

"No, no, no. Now stop this!" Adams barked.

The constant interruptions had begun to distract the old lawyer.

The only solution was to meet with Cinque and talk it out face-to-face.

The next day, in chains, Cinque stood in Adams's doorway, flanked by U.S. marshals.

"Unshackle him," Adams said.

"Sir," the guard protested, "I'm under strict orders—"

Adams made his voice even more calm, more commanding, and repeated, "I said, unshackle him."

They walked into the greenhouse, Adams, the ex-president, and Cinque, the ex–rice farmer. No other visitor had been more attentive than Cinque to the *phalaenopeis* from China or the *salix caprea* from France. He followed behind as Adams talked about his beloved flowers. They paused for a long time before the Blush Noisette—the now healthy roses that had grown from the cutting that Adams had taken from the Capitol gardens. Before another potted plant, a green prickled one, Cinque said, "aloe" in Mende. Adams nodded. "Yes, African aloe."

They had much in common despite their differences. They also had much to discuss. They took seats on a greenhouse bench, with Covey there to translate.

"Do you know who I am?" Adams asked.

107

"Yes. You are a chief."

"*Was* a chief."

"A chief can't become anything less than a chief. Even in death," Cinque explained, wondering how it could be any different here in America.

Adams looked beyond the two of them, remembering his years as the American president. "I only wish it were true here, Cinque.

"One tries to govern wisely, in a way that betters the lives of one's villagers. One tries to 'kill the lion.'" He glanced at Cinque. "Unfortunately, one isn't always wise enough. Or strong enough. Cinque, we are about to bring your case before the highest court in our land. We are about to do battle with a lion that is threatening to rip our country in two. And all we have is a rock."

Cinque struggled to understand the man's words, what he meant. His doubts began to increase. "Is he going to be any help at all?" he asked Covey.

"What did he say?" Adams wanted to know.

"I didn't catch it," Covey said.

Adams resumed. "I'm being honest with you. The task ahead of us is an exceptionally difficult one."

Cinque interrupted. "We won't be going in there alone."

Looking at Baldwin, Adams said, "Indeed not.

We have 'right' at our side. We have 'righteousness' at our side. We have *Baldwin* over there." Adams's tone made it clear he worried that there wasn't enough right and righteousness or Baldwin to win against the president and his power to influence U.S. Supreme Court justices.

"I meant my ancestors," Cinque said. "I will call into the past, far back to the beginning of time, and beg them to come help me at the judgment."

He paused to look intensely at the old man. "And they must come. For at this moment, I am the whole reason they have existed at all."

Now Adams struggled to understand. A long moment of silence followed as Adams wondered about Cinque's words. When the truth finally came to him, it hit him with more force and power than any of the law books he had ever read in his life.

A week later, the Supreme Court opened to hear the last appeal in the case of the United States versus the *Amistad* Africans.

25

Outside the Supreme Court building in Washington, D.C., pro-slavery and anti-slavery crowds shouted taunts and threats to one another as the military guardsmen stood by. Inside, John Quincy Adams prepared to begin his four hours of argument before the largest court bench in America.

Behind the mahogany bench sat the nine justices, with Chief Justice Roger Brooke Taney at the center. Five of the nine were from the South. Three of the five owned slaves. All of them, Adams suspected, might have been influenced by President Van Buren.

It had been thirty years since he'd argued a case before the Supreme Court. His voice had grown weaker. His eyes watered. His hands shook. He had enemies on the bench. How could he convince them? How best could he present the truth—that the Africans held in prison were *people,* not property—before a court in a land where people still owned slaves?

The courtroom was packed with onlookers, friends and foes of the Africans. The upcoming trial had become an international news story. As Adams stood up to speak, he felt all the world was looking at America that day.

"This is the most important case ever to come before this court," he said, "because what it in fact concerns is the very nature of man."

Adams entered into evidence the letters that had passed between the nine-year-old queen and the American president. He revealed also Van Buren's orders to the *Grampus.* Finally, he read from an article written by a Southern politician, John Calhoun, who believed that slavery was "neither sinful nor immoral. Rather—as war and antagonism are the natural states of man—so, too, is slavery."

Adams paused a long moment, holding the article in his hand. Then he spoke again.

"Gentlemen, I must say I differ with the author of this article, and with our president: the natural state of mankind is, instead, *freedom.*"

He looked back at Cinque, the only one of the Africans present in the courtroom.

111

"And the proof is the lengths to which a man will go to regain it once taken. He will break loose his chains. He will decimate his enemies. He will try, and try, and try—against all odds, against all adversity—to get home."

Adams walked over to Cinque and asked him to stand. He wanted every eye in the court to look at the regal young man. The room remained dead silent for a long while.

"This man is black," Adams finally said. "We can all see that. But can we also see as easily what is equally true. That he *alone* is the only true hero in this room?

"If he were white, he wouldn't be standing before this court, fighting for his life. If he were white and his enslavers British, he wouldn't be able to stand, so heavy the weight of the medals we would bestow upon him. Songs would be written about him. The great authors of our time would fill books about him. His story would be told and retold in our classrooms. Our children—because we would make sure of it—would know his name as well as they know Patrick Henry's!"

His voice grew more and more powerful as his speech continued. Adams crossed the room again. This time, he stood before a framed reproduction of the Constitution of the United States. "Yet, if the

South is right, what are we to do with this embarrassing document? And what of this one?" He pointed to the Declaration of Independence. "'All men are created equal . . . inalienable rights . . . life, liberty' and so on and so forth. What on earth are we to do with this?"

Adams tore up the paper in his hand and let the pieces flutter to the floor.

Adams told the court about his conversation with Cinque, how Cinque and the other Mende believe that they could summon the spirit of their ancestors. The ancestors' wisdom and strength could aid them in situations where there appeared no hope at all. Then Adams looked up to more framed hangings, the wall of imposing portraits. His ancestors. America's forefathers.

"Thomas Jefferson, Benjamin Franklin, James Madison, Alexander Hamilton, George Washington . . ." The ex-president paused before the portrait of his own father, the second president of the United States. "John Adams."

He stared at the portraits and finally addressed his remarks to them. "We desperately need your strength and wisdom to triumph over our fears, our prejudices, ourselves. Give us the courage to do what is right. And if it means civil war—*then let it come.* And when it does, may it be, finally, the last battle of the American Revolution."

His words echoed in the room, then faded away. In complete silence, he turned and strode past the nine justices and returned to his chair.

"And that's all I have to say," Adams concluded.

Outside, a light snow had begun to fall.

26

Heavy snow had fallen all evening. The roads leading to the Supreme Court were treacherous for travelers. Yet, that next morning, on the day that the decision about the *Amistad* Africans would be announced, even more people squeezed into the Supreme Court chambers.

The nine justices, their faces impassive, watched the gathering crowd—the attorneys for both sides, the lone prisoner Cinque, the opposing forces. Then, Justice Story, reading the majority decision, began to speak.

"In the case of the United States of America versus the *Amistad* Africans, it is an opinion of this court that our treaty of 1795 with Spain, on which the prosecution has primarily based its arguments, is inapplicable."

Covey whispered the translation to Cinque.

"We are left then with the decision: that these particular Africans are not slaves, and therefore cannot be considered merchandise, but are rather free individuals. With certain legal and moral rights, including the right to engage in insurrection against those who would deny them their freedom.

"Therefore, it is our judgment, with one dissention—that the defendants are to be released from custody at once, and, if they so choose, be returned to their homes in Africa."

The justice banged the mallet to close the case.

◆ ◆ ◆

As the manacles fell away from Cinque's wrists, he looked up at John Quincy Adams who stood before him. "What did you say? What words did you use to persuade them?"

"Yours" was Adams's simple reply. The two men shook hands.

Theodore Joadson extended his hand. But instead of shaking hands, Cinque deposited the small charm into Joadson's palm.

"To keep you safe," said Cinque.

Then he noticed Roger Baldwin, standing apart, waiting, unsure—and he walked to him and offered his hand.

"Thank you," Cinque said in English.

Baldwin did not shake it. He grasped the hand and held it to his heart. *"Bi sie, Sengbe,"* said Baldwin in Mende.

27

It was dusk at Lomboko, the slave factory where Cinque and the others had been loaded onto the *Tecora* two long years before. A guard glanced across the bay from his lookout in the tower. He could see a ship in the failing light, but he couldn't quite make out its flag. Until the ship drew nearer and then he recognized it—the Union Jack!

By that time, the red line of British sailors had already stormed the gates. They aimed their muskets with precision at the startled slavers and guards of the slave factory and began to fire. The guard in the tower reached for his musket, but he was too late.

The soldiers smashed open the prison cells, releasing stunned Africans who had been captured and imprisioned like Cinque and the other *Amistad* Africans had so many months before. Some of the old and weak captives were unable to walk, but they were helped to their freedom by the British marines.

Captain Fitzgerald, the British naval officer who had testifed on behalf of the Africans weeks before, waited on his ship anchored just offshore. When he received the all-clear signal from his first mate, he gave the final order.

"Fire!" the captain said calmly. In response to this quiet command, cannons thundered one after the other. They hit their targets. A cell exploded, the iron bars and splintering timbers becoming clouds of dust and smoke.

Soon after, the guard tower crashed to the ground in flames.

◆ ◆ ◆

Crossing the Atlantic under full sail, its prow slicing though the waves, the American merchant ship *The Gentleman* carried the Africans back toward their homes—all but Yamba, who that day was being baptized in a New England church.

All along the deck, the Africans stood: Kimbo, Grabo, Buakei and Maseray, all the others, including the girls and the little boy, no longer in American clothes, and James Covey, no longer in his British uniform.

119

Cinque, standing at the bow, stared straight ahead. He watched the horizon where the sun, low in the sky, pinpointed their destination.

He heard her again—his wife, calling to him in the plaintive Mende chant. Her voice seemed to come from the land that lay before him, Africa, still too distant to see, but a place that waited there like a promise fulfilled.

◆ ◆ ◆

Behind him, behind them all, in America, in the years that followed, other voices cried out. Pro-slavery. Anti-slavery. Harsh. Vehement. Followed a generation later by the sharp retort of musket shots as armies of Union blue and Confederate gray clashed on the battlefield.

The "last battle of the American Revolution"— the Civil War—had begun.

About the Author

Joyce Annette Barnes lives with her family in Smyrna, Georgia. She is the author of two critically acclaimed novels for young readers: *The Baby Grand, the Moon in July, and Me* and *Promise Me the Moon.*